BRADFORD TROLLEYBUSES
THE FINAL YEARS

David Christie

AMBERLEY

First published 2019

Amberley Publishing
The Hill, Stroud
Gloucestershire, GL5 4EP

www.amberley-books.com

Copyright © David Christie, 2019

The right of David Christie to be identified as
the Author of this work has been asserted in
accordance with the Copyrights, Designs and
Patents Act 1988.

ISBN 978 1 4456 9479 5 (print)
ISBN 978 1 4456 9480 1 (ebook)

British Library Cataloguing in Publication Data.
A catalogue record for this book is available from
the British Library.

Origination by Amberley Publishing.
Printed in the UK.

Contents

Introduction

Bradford's trolleybus system was the last to operate in Britain, closing on 26 March 1972. It was also the first to open, along with Leeds, but their system was abandoned in 1928. Some 47 route miles were operated at its peak (1961), with the last new route being opened, to Holme Wood, as late as 1960.

From 1961 onwards however, some route closures were made coinciding with the departure (to Sheffield) of the General Manager, the delightfully named Chaceley T. Humpidge, who had been a great advocate for electric traction. The Bradford topography was ideally suited to electric traction, with most routes involving a protracted climb out of the city.

Routes are shown below as of mid-1967, the Bradford numbering showing short workings as separate route numbers:

Route 6:   Thornbury–City–Four Lane Ends–Springhead Road
Route 7:   Thornbury–City–Four Lane Ends–Springhead Road–Thornton
Route 8:   City (Sunbridge Road)–Whitby Road–Duckworth Lane Infirmary
Route 16: City (Sunbridge Road)–Four Lane Ends–Allerton
Route 37: City (Thornton Road)–Pasture Lane–Clayton
Route 38: City (Thornton Road)–Pasture Lane
Route 40: City (Forster Sq.)–Peel Park–Bolton Junction–Five Lane Ends–Thackley Corner–Saltaire
Route 41: City (Forster Sq.)–Peel Park–Bolton Junction–Five Lane Ends–Thackley Corner
Route 42: City (Forster Sq.)–Peel Park–Bolton Junction–Five Lane Ends–Greengates
Route 43: City (Forster Sq.)–Peel Park–Bolton Junction–Five Lane Ends
Route 44: City (Tyrell St)–Little Horton–St Enochs Road
Route 45: City (Tyrell St)–Little Horton–St Enochs Road–Wibsey
Route 46: City (Tyrell St)–Little Horton–St Enochs Road–Buttershaw

The eastern routes terminating at Greenshaw, Tong, Bradford Moor and Eccleshill had been closed in the period from 1961 to early 1967, including the newest (Holme Wood spur), which only lasted seven years. The north-west Crossflatts route beyond Saltaire closed in 1963.

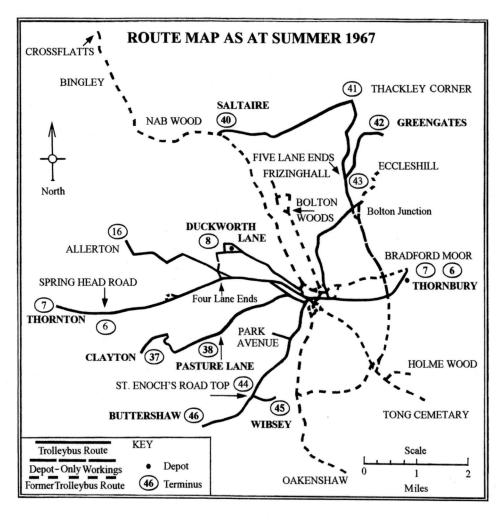

In the route map above, the routes photographed in this book are shown in bold. (Map courtesy of Graham R. Jelly)

The book starts with a single photograph taken near Saltaire in 1967, which was my very first trolleybus photo. This was purely a 'one-off' as I was passing with a non-bus friend, intent on matters railway. Exactly why this did not trigger a proper visit is lost in the mists of time, but other priorities took precedence and it was not until 25 April 1969 that this state of affairs was remedied. The date was just five days after the Bournemouth trolley closure so that was certainly incentive enough. On that first proper visit, the town centre was the obvious start, followed by investigating the various 'inner' route wiring junctions. It wasn't until my next August 1970 trip that I discovered the outer route sections and their climbs out of the city. I was also able to find the routes where original-bodied vehicles were used.

The next visit was in May 1971, armed with a new camera and accompanied by my nine-year-old nephew. Only one trolley terminus (Thornton) was photographed, along with the city centre.

Then to the last weekend, taking in the closure on 26 March 1972. Coming from the south (Romford, Essex), arrival was not until late Friday night, this time with two fellow enthusiasts. Thornbury depot and Thornton terminus were well covered on the Saturday, with the last tours at Four Lane Ends, Springhead Road, Thornton and the city being covered on the Sunday.

The fleet as of 1967, with ninety-six vehicles, was as follows:

703–714: 1945; Karrier W/East Lancs. Rebodied 1960, front-entrance.
715–719: 1945; Karrier W/East Lancs. Rebodied 1957, rear-entrance.
720–739: 1946; Karrier W/East Lancs. Rebodied 1958, fifteen front-entrance, five rear-entrance.
740–751: 1949; BUT 9611T/Roe.
752–759: 1950/1; BUT 9611T/Weymann.
775–784: 1945/6; Karrier W/East Lancs. Rebodied 1956, rear-entrance. Ex–Llanelli & District, 1956.
785–793: 1943/4; Karrier W/East Lancs. Rebodied 1958/9, front-entrance. Ex-Darlington (single-deck), 1956.
794–801: 1950/1; BUT 9611T/East Lancs. Ex-St Helens, 1959.
831–835: 1949; BUT 9611T/East Lancs. Rebodied 1962, front-entrance. Ex-Doncaster, 1962.
841–847: 1948–50; Sunbeam F4/East Lancs. Rebodied 1962/3, front-entrance. Ex-Mexborough & Swinton, 1962.

Depots were at Thornbury and Duckworth Lane.

Please note that all rebodied trolleys are shown with the body dates, and all are front-entrance unless otherwise stated.

Saturday 17 June 1967

On the outskirts of Bradford, No. 792, a 1959 rebodied vehicle, heads to the extremity of the system at Saltaire on route 40. Note the vending machines on the shop wall.

Friday 25 April 1969

On my first 'proper' visit, in typical spring weather, trolleybus No. 714 (1960) on the 6 route lines up with Leyland PD2 bus No. 572 after a shower at the town hall roundabout.

Trolleybus No. 714 now leaves the roundabout on its way to the eastern terminus at Thornbury. The modern furniture store here was a bit of an eyesore!

Ex-St Helens trolley No. 799 (1951), showing how well this original-bodied batch blended in with Bradford's East Lancs rebodied vehicles. No. 718 (1957) is behind. Each trolley is on one of the two remaining southern routes – Nos 46 and 45 – and they are shown here near the town hall.

A solo shot of ex-St Helens No. 799 at the town hall roundabout on route 46, bound for Buttershaw.

1958-bodied No. 785, seen at the same spot on route 46, showing that much demolition had been carried out here.

In contrast to the St Helens vehicles, Bradford's own trolleys from 1950 had curvaceous Weymann bodies, as displayed here by No. 753, seen entering the roundabout on Route 45.

No. 753 pulls out of Tyrell Street into the roundabout – now on route 46. The Weymann body shows an interesting feature – a glass panel on the nearside, by the wheel arch. Only this particular trolley was so treated. Enormous cranes tower over the scene at this spot.

Almost identical, even to the adverts, are 1958-bodied Nos 788 and 785, seen here at Little Horton Lane on route 46. The rear trolley is about to return to its depot.

On route 45, Weymann trolley No. 753 enters the roundabout by the hoardings.

The last image of the town centre on this day shows No. 753 again, navigating the daffodils and flower beds of the town hall roundabout on route 45 for Wibsey.

A depot view at Thornbury depot of Weymann-bodied No. 757 (1951). This standard version did not carry the lower nearside glass panel.

Trolleybus No. 713 (1960) passes the depot at Thornbury on route 7.

Trolleybuses at Thornbury depot, with 1959-bodied No. 792 and 1963-bodied No. 846. The latter is one of the most recent type with a larger windscreen – although that detail is not that discernible in this shot.

No. 731 (1958) passes through the junction near Laisterdyke, nearing the terminus of route 7 at Thornbury. The wires to the right are used for depot workings only.

Above: Trolley No. 727 (1958) negotiates the complex crossing at Bolton Junction on route 40. This view shows one of the rarer rear-entrance rebodied types. This particular example also had unusual bumper bars at the rear.

Opposite: Ex-St Helens trolley No. 801 at Bolton Junction amid sunny intervals and stormy skies!

Weymann-bodied No. 758 (1951) turning left at Bolton Junction on the Saltaire route.

Ex-St Helens No. 801 passes 1956-bodied rear-entrance trolley No. 775 on route 40 at Bolton.

A change to the west of the city, at Four Lane Ends, with 1960 No. 713 on route 7.

Above: Trolley No. 792 (1959) at Five Lane Ends on route 40.

Opposite: 1958 trolley No. 787 near Idle on route 40.

Friday 7 August 1970

A late afternoon arrival in Bradford enabled a quick look in at Thornbury depot – where Weymann-bodied No. 758 had just arrived, joining 1956-bodied No. 784.

Weymann No. 758 arriving at Thornbury depot.

A night-time view at Thornbury depot.

Saturday 8 August 1970

Opposite: The day dawned sunny but misty, and here Roe-bodied No. 745, one of a batch of twelve from 1949, climbs by Eccleshill on route 40. Seen several times during the day, No. 745 was the only Roe-bodied trolley found in service.

At Five Lane Ends, 1959 trolley No. 789 heads for town on route 42.

1962-bodied trolley No. 834 – one of the deeper-windscreen types – at Bolton Junction.

Trolleys Nos 790 and 791 (1959) pass each other on route 42 at Bolton Junction.

Another 1962-bodied trolley; this time, No. 831 is stopped at the traffic lights at Bolton on route 42.

Roe-bodied No. 745 on route 42 near Idle, with typical (hazy) views over the valley.

1962-bodied No. 844 arrives at Idle on route 40. Note the rather unusually sited zebra crossing!

Trolley No. 831 (1962) passes through the gap between the church and the pub at Idle.

Roe trolley No. 745 again, in a much closer view near Five Lane Ends on route 40, showing damage to its nearside corner.

No. 745 is now seen at the route 40 terminus of Forster Square, the modern tower blocks providing a different atmosphere to the more familiar Town Hall Square. These buildings have since been demolished. My car, a Hillman Imp Californian parked on the left, creeps into the image.

Ex-St Helens No. 799 was another original-bodied trolley seen about on that day. It is seen here at the town hall roundabout on route 46 to Buttershaw. Note that the construction work shown on page 11 in 1969 has now resulted in yet another large tower block. This building was demolished in 2002.

St Helens No. 799 at Town Hall Square, the angle to the right of the previous picture managing to cut out the modern building.

Another Ex-St Helens vehicle – No. 795, near Wissey on route 45. This trolley seems to have suffered more than No. 745 in regards to body damage.

St Helens No. 799 seen near Wibsey, on route 46 to Buttershaw.

Wibsey roundabout with St Helens No. 799 closely followed by a Regent V bus from a batch used for trolleybus replacement.

St Helens trolley No. 795 is seen at Wibsey, the terminus of route 45.

No. 795 now turns on the circle at Wibsey.

The other terminus to have a large turning circle was Pasture Lane, 2 miles north-west of Wibsey, on route 38, which was a short working of the Clayton route. Here, Weymann-bodied No. 758 is seen arriving and taking the circle.

Weymann No. 758 at the Pasture Lane terminus of route 38.

No. 758 now leaves Pasture Lane on its way back to the city.

No. 758, seen passing 1958 trolley No. 738. This was a shot taken through my car's windscreen.

No. 758 back at the town hall roundabout.

Both images: Lidget Green crossroads, a short distance from the Pasture Lane terminus of route 38, with Weymann No. 758 again.

Rear-entrance No. 782 (1956) nears the terminus of route 37 at Clayton.

Above: The Thornton terminus of route 7, with 1960 trolley No. 709 departing.

Opposite: Trolley No. 734 (1958) about to turn into the turning circle at Thornton.

Duckworth Lane, the terminus of route 8, with two unidentified 'standard' trolleys.

Roe trolley No. 745 finished for the day at Thornbury depot.

Opposite: Town Hall Square by night, with trolley No. 721 (1959) on route 7.

Saturday 8 May 1971

On my return to the city the next year, the trainer trolleys were much in evidence in the centre – such as No. 063 (ex-No. 746), one of the few remaining Roe-bodied vehicles. It is seen here with the backdrop of the Bradford Exchange station, which closed in 1973 and was demolished three years later.

Another view of No. 063 at the Market Street/Charles Street corner.

Roe-bodied No. 745 had been a much-photographed trolley in service on my last visit but had now joined the trainer fleet, albeit keeping its normal fleet number (the trainers were numbered in a '0' series) and displaying only the statutory 'L' card. The damaged nearside wing, seen in 1970, had been tidied up a bit – but a bent panel on the offside was now apparent. No. 745 is seen here at the town hall roundabout with the flower beds still looking good and the hoardings in front of the 'Alhambra' and Odeon still standing.

Trainer No. 063 passes the (by now) completed new building (since demolished!) at the town hall roundabout.

Both Roe trainers are seen here together with No. 063 passing No. 745 at the stop. Rebodied No. 793 is also at the stop. The twin towers of the Odeon building are prominent. The Odeon closed in 2000 but is now undergoing restoration.

Town Hall Square, with 1956 rear-entrance trolley No. 782 on route 37. One of the replacement buses, No. 202, is seen passing.

1959-bodied No. 728 at the city terminus of route 8.

Trolley No. 721 (1959), on route 45, follows a West Yorkshire bus near the town hall. My nine-year-old nephew looks on.

No. 721 turns out of Market Street, while the West Yorkshire bus can now be seen to be a 1965-registered Lodekka. In front of this is trolley No. 785.

1958-bodied No. 726 on route 7 at a neat and tidy town hall roundabout.

The two Roe trainers parked with poles down in Thornton Road. Note the wheel chock under No. 063's wheel.

Similar at first glance to the shot above, here we see St Helens No. 795 in service on route 38. It is passing the Roe trainer, presenting an interesting comparison between body styles.

A last look at the Roe pair from the pavement.

Trolley No. 844 (1962) leaves Forster Square roundabout on route 40. This vehicle was looking good, having undergone a repaint.

No. 835, another of the modern batch, is seen on route 42, leaving Forster Square. The '60s buildings are well shown here – all have since been demolished.

Rear-entrance No. 719 (1957) at Forster Square on the 42 Greengates route.

1959 trolley No. 739 nears the terminus of route 7 at Thornton. This shot was taken from my car.

No. 739 now departs Thornton. Note the ancient AEC Mammoth lorry at the left of the picture – a rare find at this date.

One of the few rear angle shots that I took of a rear-entrance rebodied trolley; in this instance it is No. 777, seen arriving at the Clayton terminus of route 37. This 1956-bodied trolley doesn't have the bumper bars at the rear that were seen fitted to No. 727 on page 19.

St Helens No. 785 at the Pasture Lane terminus of route 38. This was the only original-bodied trolley seen in service that day.

As we were staying the night in Bradford, the opportunity was taken to try for a few night scenes. Here is No. 709 (1960) at the city terminus of route 8. Traffic lights, a handy pole to lean on and a hand-held exposure of one second sufficed to capture the shot.

Another handy traffic light enabled me to capture No. 735 (1959) on an uphill stretch of Sunbridge Road, near the route 8 terminus.

Opposite: Rear-entrance No. 777 on the 37 route at Town Hall Square. The clock tower bells regaled us with the *Dr Kildare* theme! This shot was taken at half-a-second exposure.

Sunday 9 May 1971

A Sunday morning ride was taken on a route 40 trolley. This is the view near Idle.

Passing trolley No. 792 near Five Lane Ends on route 40. This image was taken from the upper deck of a trolley.

Trolleybus No. 705, near Manningham on route 8. This shot was taken from the car on our way out of Bradford.

Friday 24 March 1972

We arrived late on Friday for the last weekend, fortunately in time to see No. 712 finishing one of the last service workings at Duckworth Lane depot.

Saturday 25 March 1972

On this penultimate day, five pre-booked specials operated by three vehicles were being run over part of the system. The first of these, trolley No. 712, is seen here leaving Thornbury depot. Stopped at the kerb is a reminder of the Bournemouth system (closed in April 1969), with preserved Leyland Tiger PS2 No. 88 dating from 1950.

Weymann No. 758 was splendidly presented on Thornbury's forecourt. She is now preserved and this image was chosen by her owners, the Bradford Trolleybus Association, to head their home page on their website.

The depot cat has finished its inspection.

Weymann No. 758 on display at Thornbury depot.

Also on display on the forecourt was repainted No. 737, which was destined for the Bradford Industrial Museum.

The second tour trolley, No. 706, is seen in the Thornton Road.

A call in at the Duckworth Lane depot was made, where the back-up decorated trolley, No. 845, was found. She had been partly repainted and had her booms hung with flags.

Trolley No. 706 at the town hall roundabout. The tours covered a limited part of the system out to Four Lane Ends, Duckworth Lane, to the west and Thornbury to the east.

No. 712 in Park Road, Thornton.

This double-page sequence taken at Thornton terminus shows two tours, with No. 712 departing and No. 706 arriving.

Trolley No. 706 waits to leave Thornton terminus.

No. 706 was duly caught up with in Thornton Road.

The next spot reached in time to photograph No. 706 was at the Duckworth Lane roundabout.

Another 'windscreen shot', this time of No. 712 on Whetley Hill as it headed back to town.

In the city centre, with No. 712 at Bank Street.

No. 712 at the Exchange station. The following moped seemed to be unavoidable.

Back at Thornbury depot now to see the tour trolleys return. We were treated to an incident when trolley No. 846 arrived. Unfortunately the driver forgot his special instructions to take the turn into the depot where the frog was being manually operated by the personnel on the tower wagon. This resulted in dewirement and breakage of the trolleyheads, which showered down onto a following car's bonnet, an irate lady car driver and a shamefaced trolley driver subsequently being marched into the office.

No. 706 arriving at Thornbury depot off its tours – with No. 737 still on static display.

The errant No. 846 now safely in the old tram workshop, complete with tracks. No. 846 wasn't one of the tour trolleys so it was probably being transferred from Duckworth Lane.

Trolley No. 706 enters the depot in diminishing light.

The last shot of the day, showing the partly decorated No. 846 being transferred to Thornbury. No. 846 had not been used on tours this Saturday but would on the morrow.

Sunday 26 March 1972

The final day of operation began with sunny intervals, which soon became few and far between. Eight trolleys were running today, plus the last one of all – No. 844.

Above: On one of the early tours, No. 844's back-up, sister No. 845, is seen here at Four Lane Ends.

Opposite: No. 706 near Four Lane Ends. The mill shown on the left was demolished in the last few years.

Trolley No. 846 again, this time in Springhead Road. The tours were running to Thornton today.

The Squire Lane depot-only section was being used today, and here we see No. 706 climbing the hill. Way in the distance the visiting Bournemouth Tiger turns at the junction.

Opposite: A general view of the centre by the town hall with No. 845 emerging into Bridge Street.

Trolley No. 706 pulls out of Hall Ings into Bridge Street.

Most of the tour trolleys are seen here from my car: Nos 843, 712, 706, 713, 703 and 845.

Springhead Road, featuring trolley No. 711.

No. 713 near the Thornton terminus.

No. 843 approaches Thornton terminus, this shot showing the old railway viaduct yonder.

Trolley No. 713 in Leeds Road.

Leeds Road by Laisterdyke, with No. 713 climbing out of the city.

The last tours at Thornbury, with trolley No. 735 passing Nos 712, 843 and 713.

The sun hadn't deserted us entirely as No. 712 heads off with No. 735 waiting.

Above: With 'Bradford's' on the offside and 'Britain's' on the nearside, No. 844 is seen turning out of Hall Ings to take up the last run.

Next page: No. 844 in Bridge Street. She was closely followed by a tower wagon, which I would have preferred to see distantly.

No. 844 stopped at the town hall to pick up the VIPs.

No. 844 pulls away from Town Hall Square.

No. 844 and its entourage in Thornton Road.

A closer view of No. 844 shows what a good job they had made of the special livery.

No. 844 back in the city centre by the Exchange station.

The scene inside Thornbury depot with No. 844, after the last rites and speeches.

Trolleys Nos 703, 842 and 846 lined up inside.

The sun returned for the last shot of the day – of No. 737 by the old tram shed.

24 June 1972
Three months later, on Saturday 24 June 1972, I was back in Bradford and looked in at Thornbury. At that moment Weymann trolley No. 758 was in the process of being moved prior to being collected for preservation – a chance meeting indeed! The middle picture shows No. 758 being towed outside the depot building by the works' Land Rover.

Preserved Bradford Trolleybuses

All images in this section have been kindly supplied by my friend Graham Jelly who, living in Nottingham, is in a much better position than I for visiting the two sites shown.

Roe-bodied No. 746 (1949), now resplendent in its original livery, photographed at Sandtoft Trolleybus Museum in April 2007.

No. 746 again, but this time appearing at an event at the Black Country Museum at Dudley in June 2000.

Trolley No. 792 (1959) at Sandtoft in September 2018.

Trolley No. 735 (1959) at Dudley in June 1998. Note the rear bumpers. The Dudley events took place every two years between 1992 and 2008 with visiting trolleybuses running on the Dudley wiring during June.

Trolley No. 792 at Dudley in June 2002.

Trolley No. 844 (1962) at Dudley in June 2004.

Preserved Bradford Trolleybuses – The List

515: 1913; Single-deck (body only), un-restored(?). Bradford Industrial Museum.

562: 1929; Single-deck, had been used as a caravan. Sandtoft Trolleybus Museum. To be restored.

703: 1945; Karrier W/East Lancs. Rebodied 1960. West of England Transport Collection, Winkleigh, Devon.

704: 1945; Karrier W/East Lancs. Rebodied 1960. East Kent Railway, Shepardswell, Kent.

706: 1945; Karrier W/East Lancs. Rebodied 1960. Sandtoft Trolleybus Museum. In working condition.

711: 1945; Karrier W/East Lancs. Rebodied 1960. West of England Transport Collection, Winkleigh, Devon.

735: 1945; Karrier W/East Lancs. Rebodied 1959. Black Country Museum. Repainted into Walsall livery.

737: 1945; Karrier W/East Lancs. Rebodied 1959. Bradford Industrial Museum.

743: 1949; BUT/Roe. Sandtoft Trolleybus Museum. Awaiting restoration.

746: 1949; BUT/Roe. Sandtoft Trolleybus Museum. In original livery and in working condition.

758: 1951; BUT/Weymann. Bradford Trolleybus Society (almost fully restored), Keighley Bus Museum.

770: 1949; BUT/Weymann. (Ex-Notts & Derby). West of England Transport Collection. In N&D livery.

792: 1944; Karrier W/ East Lancs. Rebodied 1959. Sandtoft Trolleybus Museum. In working condition.

799: 1951; BUT/East Lancs. (Ex-St Helens). Sandtoft. Preserved in original St Helens livery and working.

834: 1949; BUT/ East Lancs. Rebodied 1962. Sandtoft Trolleybus Museum. In working condition.

844: 1948; Sunbeam F4/ East Lancs. Rebodied 1962. W. Yorks PTE. On loan to Keighley Bus Museum.

845: 1950; Sunbeam F4/ East Lancs. Rebodied 1963. Sandtoft Trolleybus Museum. Not on display.

846: 1950; Sunbeam F4/East Lancs. Rebodied 1963. Sandtoft Trolleybus Museum. Not on display.

847: 1950; Sunbeam F4/East Lancs. Rebodied 1963. Sandtoft Trolleybus Museum. Not on display.

All the rebodied examples above have front entrances. Unfortunately, there are none of the rebodied rear-entrance types preserved.

Sandtoft Trolleybus Museum is the best place to see working Bradford trolleybuses (they have at least four in working condition), with around thirty opening days during their season from April to November.

A St Helens (1951) trolley in its original livery, which ran for Bradford as their No. 799. It is pictured here at Sandtoft by Graham in June 2006.